The Nature Kid's Guide to ARMADILLOS

Level 2

DAVID ANDERSON

LP Media Inc. Publishing
Text copyright © 2026 by LP Media Inc.
All rights reserved.

For information address LP Media Inc. Publishing,
30012 Variolite St NW, Princeton MN 55371
www.lpmedia.org

Publication Data

Armadillos
The Nature Kid's Guide to Armadillos — First edition.

Summary: "Learn all about Armadillos, the Nature Kid Way"
— Provided by publisher.

ISBN: 979-8-89818-171-0

[1. Armadillos - Non-Fiction] I. Title.

Title: The Nature Kid's Guide to Armadillos

CONTENTS

DIGGING DEEP

Click, click! Sharp claws break through the earth.

Armadillos are one of the coolest animals on earth. They have hard shells, long claws, and they love to dig.

Armadillos need to live where it's warm all year. Cold weather is hard for them. Their bodies do not store much fat. They need mild weather during the winter months.

These animals love loose, sandy soil. Soft ground is perfect for digging. They make homes underground to stay cool and safe.

Armadillos live near forests and grasslands. They need places with lots of bugs to eat. Streams nearby keep the soil moist and easy to dig.

AROUND AMERICAS

Nine-banded armadillos only came to the United States about 150 years ago.

Scratch! An armadillo digs in dry leaves. It lives in Texas.

Armadillos only live in the Americas. They live from the United States all the way down to South America.

Only one type of armadillo lives in the United States. It is the nine-banded armadillo. You can find them in Texas, Florida, and many other southern states.

Most armadillos live in Central and South America. Brazil alone has many different kinds. The giant armadillo can weigh up to 70 pounds. The pink fairy armadillo is only five inches long and has a soft pink shell. The three-banded armadillo is the only kind that can roll into a complete ball!

BIG AND SMALL

Lunch time! A a giant armadillo digs into a termite mound.

Nine-banded armadillos are about the size of a house cat. They weigh between 8 and 17 pounds, about as heavy as a bowling ball!

These armadillos measure 15 to 17 inches long. Their tails add another 14 inches. Stretched out, they are as long as a baseball bat.

Giant armadillos are much bigger. They can weigh up to 70 pounds!

FUN FACT!

Pink fairy armadillos are the smallest. They are only 5 inches long and fit in your hand!

AMAZING ARMOR

Armadillo armor is very tough. It can stop some snake bites and sharp thorns!

Crack! A hard shell bumps against a log. A three-banded armadillo waddles by.

Armadillos have armor made of bony plates. Tough scales cover these plates. The plates protect their back, head, and tail. The scales are made of keratin, like your fingernails!

Armadillos also have long, curved claws. The Giant Armadillo has huge front claws. They can grow up to 8 inches long! These strong claws help them dig fast.

Armadillos have small teeth shaped like pegs. They can have up to 100 teeth! Their long, sticky tongues help catch food.

SUPER SNIFFERS

Click, click, sniff! The armadillo's feet and nose work together.

Armadillos have poor eyesight. They can only see shapes and shadows. So they use their amazing sense of smell instead!

An armadillo can smell bugs buried 8 inches underground. Their long snouts are packed with scent receptors.

They also having excellent hearing. They can even hear bugs crawling underground!

An armadillo's nose is so powerful it can smell a beetle larva buried deep in the dirt while walking right over it!

BALL UP

Click! Hard plates lock together. The three banded armadillo rolls up.

The three-banded armadillo can seal itself completely into a ball. These armadillos tuck their head and feet inside and squeeze their shell together tight.

When scared, the armadillo snaps shut fast. This hard shell keeps its soft belly safe.

Other armadillos cannot roll up. They can only press themselves flat on the ground. Their **armor** shields them from above.

A jaguars bite is so strong, it can crack an armadillo's tough shell!

BUG
BUFFET
16

Buzz! Tiny ants scatter. An armadillo digs in the dirt.

Armadillos love to eat insects. Beetles, ants, and termites are their favorites. One armadillo can eat 40,000 ants in a single meal!

They also munch on grubs and larvae. These soft baby bugs live underground. Armadillos dig them up from the soil.

Sometimes armadillos eat other foods too. They snack on berries, eggs, and small frogs. Still, bugs make up most of what they eat.

Armadillos eat fire ants. This helps farmers protect crops.

TONGUE TRICKS

Armadillos can taste sweet foods and enjoy eating ripe fruit they find on the ground!

18

Flick! An armadillo flicks its long tongue into the dirt.

Armadillos have long, sticky tongues. Their tongues can be up to 12 inches long! Gooey spit covers the tongue and makes it extra sticky.

When an armadillo finds a bug nest, it gets to work. It pokes its tongue deep into tunnels. Ants and termites stick to the goo.

The tongue also moves very fast. It can flick in and out many times per second. This speed helps armadillos slurp up hundreds of bugs in just minutes. They barely chew, swallowing bugs whole!

WATCH OUT

Snap! A twig breaks, an armadillo freezes and looks around.

Many animals hunt armadillos. Coyotes chase them. Bobcats hunt them. These **predators** have sharp teeth. They have fast legs too.

Danger can also come from the sky. Hawks and owls swoop down and attack. Eagles can grab them with strong claws.

Foxes and wild dogs will also hunt armadillos. Even black bears dig up burrows.

Armadillos must always be looking out for danger from all directions.

Jaguars hunt armadillos in South America. They are the most dangerous hunter there.

QUICK ESCAPE

Whoosh! A nine-banded armadillo sprints to the bushes.

Armadillos have several ways to escape danger. Running is often their first choice. They can sprint up to 30 miles per hour!

Hiding works well too. Armadillos squeeze into thick bushes. Sharp thorns do not hurt their tough shells.

Digging is another trick. An armadillo can dig a hole in just minutes. It disappears underground fast!

Armadillos can jump 3 to 4 feet straight up when startled by a predator!

WADDLE
WALK

Click! Tiny claws tap the ground. An armadillo waddles by.

Armadillos walk with a rolling waddle. Their short legs look clumsy and they sway side-to-side.

But they can move fast! They trot and gallop. Their strong back legs help them run.

Armadillos also swim very well. They can hold their breath for up to 6 minutes! They sometimes even walk on stream bottoms looking for food.

Armadillos gulp air to puff up. Then they float across wide rivers like little balloons!

NIGHT SHIFT

Scratch! Armadillo claws tap the dirt at dusk. Time to explore!

Armadillos are **nocturnal**. This means they are active at night. They sleep during the day in cool burrows.

When darkness comes, armadillos wake up. They spend most of the night searching for food. This search may take them up to 2 miles!

On hot summer days, armadillos stay underground. In winter, they sometimes come out during warm afternoons.

Armadillos will dig a dozen or more burrows in their territory. Their strong claws can dig a home in just minutes!

LONE RANGERS

An armadillo unrolls from it's ball. It has no friends around.

Armadillos live alone most of the time. Each one has its own **burrow**. They do not form herds or packs.

Armadillos usually meet only to mate or keep warm. Then they go their separate ways. Mothers raise babies alone too.

Young armadillos may share a burrow with their mother. But soon they leave to find their own home.

Armadillos mark their territory with scent. They rub smelly glands on trees!

FINDING FRIENDS

A male may stay near a female for several days or even months during the mating season!

Sniff! A male armadillo follows a females scent trail. It leads to her rocky den.

Armadillos mate in summer months. Females may make a soft chucking sound to show they are interested. Males then follow females for days.

Males also sniff the ground to find females. Their strong sense of smell helps them track scents from far away.

After mating, males and females separate. The mother can delay the pregnancy until she has plenty of food. Babies are then born about eight months later.

TINY PUPS

Armadillo pups can walk a few hours after birth! They stay with their mother for about six months.

Snuffle! Two tiny armadillo pups huddle in a burrow.

Baby armadillos are called pups. Nine-banded armadillos have four babies at once. All four pups look the same. They are identical quadruplets!

Newborn pups are very small. They weigh only 3 to 4 ounces. That is as heavy as a deck of cards.

Pups are born with soft skin. It feels like leather. Their eyes are open right away. But their armor is not hard yet. It takes a few weeks to get tough.

MOM
MATTERS
34

Push! Mama armadillo leads her babies into the sun.

Mother armadillos care for their babies alone. Pups stay in the burrow for the first few weeks. Mom keeps them warm and safe underground.

Pups drink their mother's milk for about 2 months. Then they start eating insects. They learn to dig for food by following their mother.

Young armadillos follow their mother at night. They learn to find bugs and grubs. After 6 to 12 months, they are ready to live on their own.

Mother armadillos can delay their baby's birth for up to two years!

ANCIENT ARMOR

Slurp! A pichi armadillo eats some beetles from under a rock.

Armadillos have lived on Earth for around 50 million years. Long ago, some armadillos were huge. Over millions of years, armadillos got smaller but kept their tough armor.

They are still changing today. Armadillos keep spreading into new places. They have moved farther north than ever before, surviving in areas their ancestors never lived.

The glyptodont was an ancient relative the size of a small car!

SPOT ONE

Tap! An armadillo's claws tap the dry ground. It sniffs for bugs.

Want to see a real armadillo in the wild? Your best chance is at dusk or dawn. Look near gardens, parks, or wooded areas. Watch quietly from a distance.

Use a flashlight with red light to see better at night. Look for small holes in lawns. Fresh dirt means an armadillo visited recently!

Never touch a wild armadillo. Stay at least 10 feet away.

Armadillos make grunting sounds while searching for food. Listen for soft snuffling noises too!

GLOSSARY

armor
A hard covering that protects an animal's body like a shield.

burrows
Tunnels or holes that animals dig underground to live in.

keratin
The hard stuff that makes up your fingernails and an armadillo's scales.

nocturnal
An animal that sleeps during the day and is awake at night.

predators
Animals that hunt and eat other animals for food.